THINK ABOUT IT...!!!
From Priest to Peace

Dedra —

Peace!

Very

3-4-07

THINK ABOUT IT...!!!
From Priest to Peace

Vern Ketter

Bloomington, IN Milton Keynes, UK

AuthorHouse™
1663 Liberty Drive, Suite 200
Bloomington, IN 47403
www.authorhouse.com
Phone: 1-800-839-8640

AuthorHouse™ UK Ltd.
500 Avebury Boulevard
Central Milton Keynes, MK9 2BE
www.authorhouse.co.uk
Phone: 08001974150

This book is a work of non-fiction. Unless otherwise noted, the author and the publisher make no explicit guarantees as to the accuracy of the information contained in this book and in some cases, names of people and places have been altered to protect their privacy.

© 2006 Vern Ketter. All Rights Reserved.

No part of this book may be reproduced, stored in a retrieval system, or transmitted by any means without the written permission of the author.

First published by AuthorHouse 01/04/06

ISBN: 1-4208-9563-X (sc)

Printed in the United States of America
Bloomington, Indiana

This book is printed on acid-free paper.

Contents

Dedication vii
Acknowledgements ix
Preface xi
Introduction xiii

1	JUST TO THINK ABOUT IT!!!	*1*
2	EDUCATION, BELIEVING, THINKING	*3*
3	UH-OH…WHERE'S GOD?	*7*
4	RELIGION, CHURCH, BIBLE	*11*
5	COMMANDMENTS, PRECEPTS, LAWS	*17*
6	SIN, GUILT, CONSCIENCE	*21*
7	SIN…OR MISTAKE?	*25*
8	PRAYER, INDULGENCES, MASS	*27*
9	BAPTISM, CONFESSION, PENANCE	*33*
10	LIFE, LOVING, LIKING	*37*
11	LOVE, COURTSHIP, MARRIAGE	*39*
12	DIVORCE	*43*
13	SEX AND SEXUALITY	*47*
14	GIFT-GIVING, PRESENCE, PRESENTS	*51*
15	TIMELY PREPARATIONS	*55*

Conclusion 61

Dedication

To Janet, my friend whom I consider the greatest blessing of my life!…without whom this book would never have come to be!!…and who has helped both of us attain a degree of happiness we never thought possible…thanx, Janet!!!!

Acknowledgements

There were many, many people whose encouragement I needed to complete this work…from former students, friends, relatives, whomever…to all those who agreed and disagreed but listened, considered and discussed with open minds the possible answers to so many unanswered questions…so as not to miss mentioning any of you who know who you are…thank you all very much!

Preface

You might need a cup of coffee while reading this material, since most of it lends itself to such a conversation. There's really no order of related topics… some are altogether unrelated, much as our casual talking is. There is a strain of God, Church, and Religion in most of the opinions expressed…they've been a big part of my life. There is an important element missing throughout…your response to any of my opinions!… hearing and reading people's experiences and thoughts is now a very interesting part of my life!

I'll put a word of caution here. If you believe your faith in Christianity (or other religion) is a little weak, with a slight fear of losing whatever faith you have, you might not want to continue reading this book. On the other hand, you could accept the challenge of thinking about these subjects, and in the process come out having a stronger faith than ever before because you gave it all some serious thought!

Please remember whatever is written here is only opinion…no way trying to convert or change you…but my thoughts have firmed up my opinions considerably just by putting them on paper…resulting in a life less fearful and more happy than I ever imagined!

If any of this writing gives you the impression that I think I "know it all"…please forgive such an impression, since most of my expressions are in the form of questions…and most of the people I've questioned and listened to, even though some of them might act like they "know it all", don't seem to have any better answers!

The whole process of searching for truth sure has been very enjoyable…just being able to think, talk, listen and read with a totally free spirit…and that's my wish for you, too!

Introduction

Someone has said that the first sentence in writing a book is the hardest part of the process.

Whew!...now that the hardest part is done, maybe the rest will come easy!...it sure took long enough to get started!

The writing style is going to be as simple as possible... maybe similar to what it might be like to just sit down and talk with you for a couple of hours...letting the thoughts and words come without worrying about the form!

For those of you who don't know me...I was born in 1929 and baptized Catholic in Kelly, Kansas... attended Catholic elementary and high school in Falls City, Nebraska...two years of Catholic College at St. Benedict's, Atchison, Kansas...two more years at St. Paul Seminary, St. Paul, Minnesota for a B.A. in Philosophy…four more years at the same place for a M.A. in Theology…ordained a Catholic priest in 1955…continued education at Catholic University of America in Washington, D.C. for one year in 1961-62 for a M.A. in Education Administration…and have now completed 50 years of more education in the school of experience…with the learning process still going on!

My growing experiences…began on a farm and then at a service station…remained a priest for 14 years as a school administrator and pastor and Air Force chaplain…married after separation from the Catholic church, attempted to help raise four stepchildren…and then divorced after 25 years, during which time I owned and managed a nursing home…and am now living with my closest female nurse friend…with the intention of staying together as long as we like each other…and enjoying our home in Chillicothe, Missouri!

That's about it for my life up to now…what follows will just be putting down the thoughts I've been wanting to share…if things don't make any sense to you or the reading gets boring, I guess you can just put the book aside! Some people agree and some disagree with these thoughts…just something to think about!

Just To Think About It!!!

First of all…if you haven't read the introduction yet, I'd really suggest that you do it now, so that you'll know where I'm coming from. This is not a lot of fiction, but the results of seventy-five years of living and thinking.

Second of all…this is not an attempt to convince any of you of anything. It's just an attempt to put on paper what I believe are some of the more important things in my life, and to make sure that my life matches what I really believe!

Third of all…my present attitude toward all churches and religion has been greatly influenced by my past life and experience…like maybe it's time for a wake-up call. I believe that all 'church-goers' are about ninety-five percent in agreement…and disagree on only about five percent in their beliefs, which seems to cause all the trouble between themselves and others.

It's kind of hard to write about any subject without having the readers understand a little bit about how I feel about the present state of churches, since churches dominate a lot of people's thinking. Despite all the good stuff that seems to be accomplished, churches and religions are the center of so much dissension, wars, murders, family breakups, so much disagreement among so many people…shouldn't that little 5% of stuff that people disagree on be considered 'peanuts' in comparison to the big picture?

So now…if you disagree with what I've written so far, you might not wish to continue. On the other hand, since I've told you that I'm not trying to convince anybody of anything, you might just want to keep reading. It might also be a good idea to re-read this first chapter because of its importance in relation to what follows. Remember…I'm writing this just to get some of my thoughts on paper and maybe give you some stuff to think about!

Education, Believing, Thinking

Josh Billings is supposed to have said, "It is better to know nothing than to know what ain't so." I agree. I've been taught so much of what just ain't so!

Think about it! If a person is brought up in a system of education that supposedly helped you learn the truth, but in the process told you that it was wrong to believe something different from what it said was true, wouldn't that be teaching you 'to believe' rather than 'to think'? I think that question is at the root of everything that I now believe about both education and religion.

Something inside of us seems to give us the drive to find out the truth about everything…beginning with the curiosity of the child to the serious search made throughout our life. I guess we're just made that way…we want to know the 'truth'! We keep digging and digging until we get to something that makes the most sense to us at the time…and that satisfies until we hear or read something that makes more sense…and so it goes even when a person reaches the ripe old age of seventy-five. If this search for truth is to be successful, it would seem that all of us need to be completely free in the process to discover everything that can be known, decide what seems the best to us…and then live by that conviction!

But now…isn't this what has happened to us in our process of growing up? Our parents try to guide us in what they believe is the right direction, and in the process we end up doing what they think is right… or else! Then a system of education teaches all it has to offer, and in the process we end up doing what it teaches is right…or else! This kind of applies to both government and the church. Is there something wrong with this picture as far as freedom to seek the truth is concerned? I guess it's taken me way too many years to find out!

So maybe this is what happens. In our youth we're 'told' what is true…and have mercy on you if you disagree with parents…or a teacher…or a pastor! The final blow comes when you are taught that such and such is not only 'wrong' but also 'sinful'…whether you believe it or not! Under this kind of fearful environment, where is the freedom to search for truth? Sound like a type of brainwashing maybe? It took me over thirty-five years to realize this for myself!

Maybe we should put down some examples. I think turmoil enters in when we examine closely what we 'really' believe…not just what we're 'told' to believe or else! Some such things are: the existence of God…creation…heaven…hell…sin…science…marriage…divorce…birth control…commandments…prayer…the institution of all churches…the Bible…eternity…the history of the church…education…money…government…and the list goes on and on and on! I've spent a lot of time on these subjects…maybe we should all try to determine what we 'really' believe.…instead of just believing what we've been 'told' to believe!

Looking in the mirror and telling ourselves what we really believe, or better yet, putting it down on paper, might be the best test of where our search for truth has progressed so far. Then if we find out that we don't 'really' live by what we 'really' believe, does that put us in a class known as hypocrits?…or maybe a puppet controlled by strings in the hands of the powers that be? Maybe we should think about it!

Uh-Oh…Where's God?

About five years ago I started writing some of my thoughts on paper, maybe just to see what it might be like, or if I could really do something like write a book. It's been kind of fun and interesting for me. It sure makes you stop and think about what you really believe and what you don't really believe, especially about things that have been a big part of your life for so many years. When I was talking to others about some of this stuff, I found myself saying so often "Think about it!"…and so from that time on, everything I put down on paper is from that point of view…just to have others think about it, and maybe come back with a few thoughts and reactions of their own!

When I first began putting down what I was thinking, I assured everybody that I believed in a God, with two major laws…loving Him above all things, and loving our neighbor as ourselves. Now, after much thinking and talking and reading, I've come to the point of wondering whether there is a God in the whole picture…maybe there really isn't a creator and maybe no afterlife…maybe we're here now and after this, that's all there is! I've got two major problems when I think about God, and I'm leaning toward a conclusion that isn't very popular with many people, but could be true even if we don't like it!

My first problem is the old question of "Where did God come from?" After you've believed and taught all the old usual answers for so many years, you get kind of tired listening to people dismiss the question with 'just look around you'…or 'you just have to accept it on faith'…is that the best we can come up with? How can we go from saying that things had to be made by a creator…to accepting so easily that the creator had no beginning? That's a very big step, and someone needs to come up with a better explanation. I'd like to state at this time that I'm certainly not against the idea of needing a creator…I just need some more convincing arguments.

My second problem concerns the matter of a creator not letting us know for sure what the truth is. If I were the creator, I believe I'd want everyone to know for sure. Some would say that we're just not supposed to know it yet, and then also that there would be no need for faith. If a creator really is, then with all the power of a creator, why wouldn't it be very simple to let John Smith know by saying "John, this is God…just want you to know I'm here…the world is all yours…use it well…be good, etc. etc." With all the modern technology we have at our disposal today for communication, God would probably have the best available. It's easy to pass the question off by saying that's just not the way it is.

I guess my conclusion to all this thinking is that there are probably two very similar myths that have been told us since birth…one is Santa Claus and the other, God…and how similar they really are! We're told of this wonderful old guy who's making a list, watching us close to see if we're being naughty or nice…who will reward us or not reward us at the end of a certain period. Very similar, no? And the reason or moral of both stories is to get us to behave, not only when we're children but also as adults…to try to get us to be nice to each other.

I was pretty disappointed when I found out there was no Santa, just as most kids are…and I am much more disappointed to be suspecting that there may not be a God, just as many of you who believe in God would also be disappointed. I think we all want God to be, with an afterlife of joy…but I'm believing at present that such is not the case, no matter how much hoping we do. There are plenty of people who will say that if there is no God, then we'd all act very bad and the world would really go to pot. I guess I really don't believe that either, because treating others well is probably the best way to go…bad guys do not have peace and happiness here on earth, as some would seem to believe.

Belief in God is a very real concern for all of us. We either believe or we don't…or we hope there is a God or there isn't. If you've got any arguments that might help me in my search for truth, I'd sure welcome your views…as long as you don't force me to accept what you believe…and not dislike me for what I believe!

Religion, Church, Bible

Think about it!...most of us probably don't spend too much time thinking about what 'religion' actually means...maybe today is a good time for it...so starting with the origin of the word itself, the Latin derivative is something like 'ligare' meaning to bind, and 're' meaning back to...so we come up with using the word 'religion' to indicate how we creatures go about the whole business of being 'bound back to' the creator... and into this picture comes 'the church' to help us with this business...and since the church kind of claims to own 'the Bible', we have quite a complex relationship developing over several hundred years...and how sure of anything can we believe translations relayed down to us through these many years, especially in the times before the printing press came into being?...and it seems so easy for the Christians to pass over such problems with statements as 'you just have to accept it on faith'!

Let's just take one example and run with it…and attempt to understand what 'the church' and its followers have done with one doctrine or belief that has been passed on since who knows when…let's consider 'ORIGINAL SIN'…who really started this story of Adam and Eve that so many accept?…and just think of all the resulting consequences that we've been just 'accepting' as facts…when we don't really have a clue…e.g.'s…the actual sin of Adam and Eve…the transferring on to all the rest of us…the beginning of shame…the inclination to do evil…baptism to remove sin from a newborn baby…confession for all the other sins we commit…the whole matter of the immaculate conception of Mary, the mother of Jesus…the virgin birth…Jesus needing to be both 'God and Man' in order to make up for original sin…the belief that the crucifixion of a son was necessary for redemption of mankind…the existence of a purgatory or hell as punishment for sin…and the offering of prayers such as the sacrifice of the mass, rosary, stations of the cross, penances, etc. in order to free others from punishment…and the limbo created for unbaptized babies…quite an impressive list of stuff we've been taught by those who have established themselves as authorities in 'religion'!

The 'church' as it exists today has come up with tons of things for us to accept…and maybe all this administrative power and real estate ownership should be up for a little examination by followers who have been giving such loyalty for so many years…why in the world would Jesus want to start another church in any way resembling the 'scribes and pharisees'?…for whom He has some serious words of reprimand…like the descriptive terms of 'hypocrits' and 'brood of vipers'… and saved such terms as 'forgiveness' and 'kindness' in His treatment of sinners…the scribes and pharisees claimed their superiority of knowledge over Jesus and no doubt all other laymen…the church today has gone far beyond such actions by giving men power to change bread and wine into the body and blood of Jesus, the power to act as intermediary in the forgiveness of sins, the master creators of regulations that bind under pain of sin, the dispenser of indulgences for some rather surprising reasons and so much of this authority based on what followers place their hopes on…the Bible!

With the ownership of the Bible claimed by the church, the next consideration might well be…the Bible!…three years of church history class and four years of Bible class, plus experience over many years, is the basis for my remarks and feelings expressed here. The writers of scripture have been declared 'inspired by God' in their writing…but are they any more inspired than I am in writing this?…(and some of you might be thinking that this is anything but inspired by God!)…and the second point to consider…think of when these writings were supposedly done and by whom and in how many different translations and into so many different languages, even before the invention of the printing press…and now think about how much trouble we have in telling or writing a true story to one another, e.g. the news media…even if it's in our own language…and now think about how the authorities have set themselves up to judge what we are free to read and what we are not to read. Some of these historical facts come out with a certain element resembling the contents of what many of us might call hogwash!…and I really don't mean to be in any way disrespectful…just factual about a subject most people have not given near enough attention to…but have just gone along the 'safe' way…accepting on faith!

With all that having been said…isn't God worthy of a much higher notion of intelligence and goodness in giving us the facts, with ability to accomplish whatever?…it seems we somehow need to glean the best of what Jesus and all the other special prophets and good guys have tried to tell us…and put out so much of the distracting, confusing, harmful material that too often compares to a story like 'santa claus' or the 'tooth fairy'...and just get back to concentrating on those two important necessities...love of God and neighbor!...think about it!

Commandments, Precepts, Laws

Think about it!...when God created us, he must have done it out of love and not to use us as playtoys...and if He wanted anything back from us, it must have been love...just like parents bring their children into this world...and about the last thing any of these parents would want from their children is a sense of fear...and if this is true, the guilt and fear that results from all the threats of sin and punishment just seem to be very uncalled for in our lives...if we were meant to love God and each other! So where did all the regulations come from?...and why?

The ten commandments of God could be up for a little questioning on our part...especially when Christ supposedly said they would all be secondary to the two most important ones, which are love of God and love of neighbor. Why don't we just stop with these two most important ones and not worry about those others. A loving God or parent would hardly set up a hell as punishment for any child who disobeyed, no matter how many mistakes they might make. Would any of you parents act any differently? Maybe we need to question the origin of these commandments, regardless of how much they have been glorified and magnified in the movie world…or by the 'churches'. We've all been taught to accept them without questioning. But how do we know how they really got transferred down to us?…and do they make that much sense? When I was only seven years old, was it right for me to learn and memorize such wonderful stuff like 'thou shalt not commit adultery' or 'thou shalt not covet thy neighbor's wife'?…and know it now or not be permitted to make my first communion!…and then be sure to examine myself on all these matters so I could make a good confession…so I can receive pardon for being however bad I was!…wouldn't it just make more sense to go to the people I may have done wrong to and tell them I'm sorry? If we spend all of our time loving God and others, we probably won't have any time left to worry about the feeling of guilt, sin, punishment and hell that results from observing all the regulations. We all need to grow up in a world believing that someone loves us…weaknesses and all…just as we are!

The six precepts of the Catholic church add to the abundance of regulations...and makes one wonder where all the people who have passed on are now...after having 'violated' the rules about going to mass on Sundays or eating meat on Fridays or fasting or contributing to the support of their pastor...since so many of these laws have apparently changed for the better. Most of the stories we have about Christ seem to indicate that He was not in favor of burdening any of us with more requirements. So much of this sounds too much like 'scribes and pharisee' stuff. It seems that 'churches' have stepped a bit out of line in the emphasizing of laws that produce guilt and fear...instead of love!

The code of canon law is probably unknown to the large majority of Christians...nevertheless its existence is real and only serves to guide and regulate all the members of the Christian community concerning a whole bushel of activities much too detailed to discuss here...and the Catholic church produces a generous amount of 'doctors of canon law' that make sure these rules are carried out in proper fashion...and perhaps serve again to complicate the life of the simple Christian who is trying so hard to just live happily, lovingly, peacefully. Some of these facts of our life seem to have an element of power-play by appointed and ordained authorities over the common layperson who is trying to make the best of this relationship...with a loving God!

The first real peace in my life came after living forty years of it…and a large part, I believe, is due to the fact that these regulations concerning my spiritual life have been relegated to the back burner, including the 'churches' that promote such…and living with love instead of fear is such a pleasant experience…think about it!

Sin, Guilt, Conscience

Think about it!…Too much concern about such a large number of commandments, precepts and laws would seem to result in the making of a person who is filled with the sense of guilt and fear of sin with every move he makes…rather than a person happy about being loved and ready to live a life of love in return. Our notion of God would be a lot more acceptable without all the laws…and would sure make a lot more sense out of the life and teachings of Jesus! There must be something causing people to lose that whole idea of a loving God and have it replaced by such stressful concepts as fear, guilt, sin, fire and brimstone, etc.!

Don't you ever kind of wonder where the whole story about Adam and Eve came from?…and because of their behavior, all the rest of us have to be cursed with some kind of inclination to do bad stuff instead of good?...and maybe worse yet, that a nice little baby is tagged with 'sin' that needs to be washed away in baptism? Why would I ever be held sinful for something my parents did? We seem to accept so much of this kind of thinking just because the Bible or church tells us so, instead of coming to some conclusions of our own about how much sense it really makes...or doesn't make! Makes one wonder why we take so much 'on faith' from all the 'smart guys'...and puts our life that results from such belief on the level of 'do it because I said so'. Which one of us hasn't squirmed a few times from such an answer to so many of our questions? Maybe it's time for adults to wonder just who they are putting their faith in, when they give an answer like 'the Bible or the church tells me so'?

I believe that the notion of guilt and sin is something we are taught and much overused as a method of disciplinary control by parents, teachers, etc. who are so often pushed to the limit on what to do next with children. Parents have so little training for such a responsibility except what tradition keeps passing on from one generation to the next...and so much passed on, not because it makes any sense, but because that's what we grew up with. Maybe you've been blessed with a life fairly preserved from the anguish caused by an exaggerated sense of guilt and sin instilled from the very first days of life.

There must be a simple answer somewhere to such problems of guilt and sin. It seems to me that the whole idea of following our conscience has been unemphasized. Such belief certainly doesn't give much credit to God for being able to deal with us so directly that we can make our decisions in life from a 'loving' standpoint, rather than that of being such a sinful creature that needs to be threatened by so many guidelines…offering a choice of 'do this or else' situation! Conscience is supposed to be that little voice within that helps us to distinguish what is good or bad. It seems that when we use our conscience to do something against what the church or other people think is the 'right' thing for us to do, then 'they' decide our conscience is warped or misguided or 'twisted'. Then, on the other hand, we've been told if we think something is wrong, even if it isn't, it's still a sin or wrong for us to do. That seems to make conscience a very important part of our life…and shouldn't it be?

With my seventy-five years of living my own personal experience and dealing with the experiences of so many others, I have really become convinced of the importance of conscience for each one of us…not a conscience 'formed' in the environment of fear, guilt, sin, discipline, purgatory, hell, etc. condition…but one that lives with some kind of assurance of a loving God directing us to live a loving life in return…think about it!

Sin…Or Mistake?

Imagine, as it might be, no personal God without all the teaching about sin, reward and punishment, no purgatory, heaven or hell or afterlife…what would that mean concerning our behavior?

If we can believe that all of us have an inclination to be loved, then it seems to me that instead of hurting each other, we would know the sense of treating each other well because if we would do so, we would get good treatment in return. If I want people to like me, I need to treat them right…if they like me, they in turn will treat me right. Doesn't that make sense?

Christianity says mistreating each other is a sin… I'm thinking maybe it's not a sin but just a plain old mistake. Good begets good…hurt begets hurt. If we

all led good lives just because it makes good sense…
rather than to receive a reward (heaven) or to avoid
punishment (hell)…wouldn't that be a better motive
for living right?

Some people want offenders to be punished in the
next life since so many get by with crime in this life. I
believe instead of calling bad behavior a sin, we need to
recognize any mistreatment of another as a mistake that
carries its own punishment after the deed right here
on Earth. Any person who hurts another by stealing,
beating, killing or abusing in any form has to live with
that offense forever…e.g. the Mafia members, all the tv
stories we watch…they pay the price of their crime in
some manner or another. Their outward appearance
may seem glorious but their inward condition is
constant stress.

Sin is always a 'mistake' but maybe it's also only a
'mistake', not a sin with consequences in an afterlife.
Most of us have felt the sting of a guilty conscience
for hurting someone somehow…so just maybe all sin
(mistakes) has its own price for to us pay, regardless
of how many bad guys seem to be getting by with
murder!

Prayer, Indulgences, Mass

Think about it!...if God is so all-important in our life, then the manner in which we might best communicate with Him ought to deserve some time for thought... and here again I can hardly hold myself back from going too fast on this machine in trying to get my thoughts on paper! One of the first requirements to make communication of any value is that it ought to be 'meaningful'. As with any of our daily conversations, we soon get tired of 'meaningless' chatter...and usually we want to move on to someone who really cares about what we say...and hopefully they know that we care about what they say. If those last couple of statements seem a little confusing, they might bear re-reading for the purpose of better understanding what we're talking about here!

When I think of all the years I spent 'saying prayers'…required or suggested…memorized…read or sung…aloud or silent…it makes me wonder where my mind was. I certainly wasn't doing a very good job of talking to God, since most of the time I seemed more concerned about doing a good performance of recitation or singing or fulfilling an obligation…rather than having a personal talk with God! I guess I never felt that I was alone with this problem. Other people seemed to have the same wandering eyes and thoughts during such times of 'prayer'…and for all practical purposes might just as well have been counting numbers to fill up the time for talking to God. That may sound a bit harsh at first, but let's just take some examples: memorized morning and evening prayers, before and after meals, before and after classes, prayers at Mass and the hours of the daily divine office, the rosary, stations of the cross, litanies, novenas, the sacraments, the Our Fathers, Hail Marys and Glory Be's. These forms and others are used in carrying out prayer rituals that have been held sacred for so long. I just think talking to God is a necessity and a wonderful thing…but shouldn't such communication be as personal between us and God as it is between ourselves?…e.g. between parent and child? What parent wouldn't rather have a simple statement of gratitude, need or love from a child…than the repetition of someone else's finest verse ten or more times in succession?…or a simple but sincere 'I'm sorry,

Mom' rather than someone else's words? I believe prayer or communication is great and necessary…but very personal…and not by rote, memorized or borrowed from someone else!

Prayers are closely connected to 'indulgences' in the Catholic church. Indulgences are the partial or full remission of punishment due to sin…time to be spent in 'purgatory' until a soul is cleansed for entry into heaven. For the saying of prayers for a certain number of times, one might get another soul released from purgatory. Sounds like a pretty good deal!…except that we have no assurance of such a thing ever happening. I think with the distraction and lack of any real communication that goes on in the repetition of formal memorized prayers, one might just as well be counting to a hundred…or several hundred! What kind of communication is actually going on with God?…and this can probably very well be said about all the times for prayer mentioned above. You readers that have never been shackled with the confinements set up by formal, written or memorized versions of prayer could very well be grateful now for being spared the problem! Think how much worse it was when some of us were required to do these religious duties in the Latin language. Who really is capable of thinking in Latin, much less read or talk it intelligibly?…some kind of real communication!

And now we come to perhaps the 'prayer of all prayers' which is known as 'the holy sacrifice of the mass'. First of all, we might do well to question how any person could give another person the power to change bread and wine into the actual body and blood of Christ. Couldn't we do well to be satisfied with all of God's marvels around us, without having to invent all the miracles and mysteries associated with the teachings about the mass, the sacraments, original sin, redemption, the trinity, indulgences, the immaculate conception of Mary, plus all the numerous other doctrines that church members are required to accept as a matter of 'faith'? Secondly, what about the continued practice of offering a certain stipend to have a mass offered for the repose of some soul…to obtain a whole or partial remission of punishment due to sin? Quite an awesome feat and it's been going on for so many years! Quite a presumption on somebody's part to teach such a thing. I believe Jesus would have a real hayday if He came to visit our churches today…perhaps somewhat similar to the hayday he had using the whip on the moneychangers in the temple!

I agree with whoever said that a sign of an educated person is the realization and admission by that person that 'he really knows so little and that he has so much more to learn'. There are so many questions to solve with our small minds…our manner of communication with God, call it prayer or whatever, with whatever effects it produces, ought to merit some of our more serious time for thought…think about it! Good luck with your efforts…it's taken me seventy-five years to get to this point…and I'm sure looking forward to learning a lot more!

Baptism, Confession, Penance

Think about it!...we've been taught that a sacrament is an outward sign instituted by Christ to give grace! This is another one of the instances that the church seems to keep adding mystery upon mystery for us to accept 'on faith'. I'm thinking this makes our relationship with God just that much more difficult...and can prompt us to ask again for more miraculous stuff...when there is really so much fantastic reality in the world to help us know our creator! The world of magic fools us so much in the entertainment sector. Wouldn't it be neat if we could just stay away from the 'holy mysterious' and stick with the ordinary stuff?

Baptism as a sacrament is supposed to wash away the stain of original sin...which we are told is there from the sin of Adam and Eve in paradise…and makes us wonder how any sin could be transferred through all the parents who ever gave birth, right down to our own parents. Then baptism is also supposed to make us a 'child of God' and 'heir to heaven'…which it seems that an innocent child in the miraculous act of birth already has a claim to. Maybe it takes several repetitions of baptizing as a priest to start thinking seriously about what is actually taking place. It takes a heap of nerve to say over an innocent baby that the devil is in any way involved in this child, brought forth in one of the greatest miracles witnessed on Earth, through the generous act of love between a woman and a man. It seems that this is just another example by the churches to add to the already too numerous mysterious rituals…presented to the faithful to accept on faith!

If the power claimed in the sacrament of baptism is not enough, how about the priestly power in the sacrament of penance, in the confessional or elsewhere? First of all you need to wonder where this power to be an intermediary between God and ourselves comes from, and then question the manner in which it is done. Teaching that all these powers came from Jesus has all the warning flags up concerning it being fact or not…coming down through all the centuries with what degree of integrity. Another thought comes up about whether we should be able to deal directly with

God, and why through anyone else…on matters that should be of concern only to God…or another person we may have offended. Here again, maybe one needs the experience of hearing confessions a thousand or more times to come to these kind of conclusions. Those of you who have never been exposed to this kind of living have another reason to be saying thanks for being spared the experience!

The idea of doing some kind of penance for the remission of your sins leaves a bit to be desired. It seems a little impractical to ask someone to say 'three Our Fathers, three Hail Marys and three Glory Be's' as a penance for a long or short list of 'sins'. In the first place, about as much thought is given to what is being said, as having the person count to three hundred and eighty-one in the case of the above penance…and in the second place, if we offended another person somehow, that person should be the recipient of our true sorrow and reparation, as the case may be. Despite all the trouble we go through in this process, we are warned that there might be an undetermined amount of punishment waiting for us in purgatory. All of this makes for a rather uneasy life of fear instead of living a life of love in return to a loving God. Then, as a natural follow-up on this kind of teaching, comes the whole matter of obtaining remission of punishment due to sin through the performance of prayers, good deeds, etc.,

etc.…in order to obtain those indulgences that have been questioned and disputed for so many centuries in the history of the church!

It's been a great relief for me to believe that we might all be better off without the church teachings on the sacraments of baptism, confirmation, holy eucharist, penance, extreme unction, holy orders and matrimony, and the sacrifice of the mass, plus all the recitations of formal prayer and mysterious rituals. I believe Jesus had a very simple formula for living that He practiced while He was on Earth…and would be the last to wish any sort of magic, any display of pomp and circumstance, power and riches, any instilling of religious fear of God instead of love…which He would find if He came to visit us again today…think about it!

Life, Loving, Liking

I believe the word 'love' may be one of the most misused and misunderstood words in the English language…I mean really misused and really misunderstood!

'Love' to me means to wish (or treat) everyone well… and the opposite is 'hate' which to me means to wish (or treat) anyone bad.

I believe that many people confuse 'love' with 'like', which I think means 'to be attracted to'…and the opposite is to 'dislike' or 'not be attracted to'. These words have nothing to do with 'love' or 'hate'!

So what's the result? To me this means we really don't have to 'like' anyone, any more than we have to 'like' sauerkraut or spinach or sports or science fiction!

To keep peace in the world, we probably have to 'love or wish well' or 'do well' to everyone no matter what despicable things we believe they have done! For the same reason, we may never 'hate or wish them evil' or 'do evil' to anyone…but we can 'dislike' them for what they do, without ever failing 'to love' and never 'to hate'!

Does that make any sense? You may have never had any problem with this in your life…but it certainly was in mine! With the daily contact we have with people, maybe it's worth some of our time to think about it!

I used to think when I disliked someone that I was committing a wrong for not loving them…and if loving everyone is so important, then I was really a bad boy… it's a great relief to be free of that fear!

There's more on love and like in the next section.

Love, Courtship, Marriage

Think about it!...of all the areas in which the word 'love' is used, it's probably most misused in the matter of romance...where the word 'like' really comes into play perhaps more importantly that we ever imagine!

If the word 'love' means to wish(treat) well...and the word 'like' means to be attracted to, wouldn't it make more sense to use the word 'like' when we are referring to our feelings for that one really special person in our life? If we are supposed to 'love' everyone, then we're really not saying anything so fantastic when we acknowledge that to someone. But if we put the word 'like' in our statement, that makes a world of difference...and so it seems that the one we 'love and like' the most, is the person for us to have that special relationship…the one we refer to as 'being in love with'!

As for some misuses of the word 'love'…think about how many times we hear people say they 'just love' this or that…such as 'I just love this coat'…or 'I just love my pickup'…or 'I just love chocolate' etc., etc., etc.…it seems the word 'like' would be more proper. When we're talking romance, if a boy tells a girl he loves her, he might be more correct to say he likes her and that would make her really someone special. It takes a while to get used to talking in these terms…but after a little practice, it sure is a lot easier, when you consider all the misuses of the word 'love' in our English language!

Courtship seems to me to be the time for determining how much a person really 'likes' another person…and to really determine that, one would have to be with that person under all different circumstances, and for a period of time…maybe for months…or years! Isn't this always the period in life when lovers try to please each other the most, in order to get the other person to 'like' them more than anyone else?…and to have that other person decide that they like you just the way you are and you like them just the way they are?

And that brings up the subject of marriage! When you consider the chances for a successful marriage isn't so good today, doesn't it sort of make you wonder who invented the whole idea of marriage? Maybe this sort of union really needs to take place in the hearts of two people…and no piece of legal paper should keep people together in a union as intimate as this. How many people are together today just because they're 'married'? If courtship is so nice, why not just keep that kind of relationship going on and on and on?

Maybe there's something wrong with the whole institution of marriage! It seems to me that something very discouraging takes place shortly after the 'I do's'! Maybe a strange sense of ownership crops up that makes people feel like they own and owe each other whatever. The whole idea of being the 'individual' that they were before marriage is lost in the shuffle! Now the constant effort of impressing and pleasing the other goes by the wayside…and the notion of 'expecting' such and such from the other sets in because 'you're mine'…and 'you owe that to me'…which seems to spoil the whole 'loving and liking' relationship needed for people to live together in such a close union!

Wouldn't it make a lot of sense, if, in the area of romance and sex and marriage, that people who get into bed together, would do so only if they 'love and like' each other a lot…and not because they 'owe' it to their partner…or they 'have to'…or they just need to 'work a little harder' at their marriage?…think about it!

Divorce

Think about it! With such a large number of marriages today ending up in the failure department, maybe it might be time to give some thought to that awful process we know as divorce. It's considered by many to be such a bad thing, but by just as many perhaps as a most beneficial happening, put off for too long in so many cases. This matter is probably best considered and written about by someone who has actual experience with divorce…not by someone who just thinks he knows what it's all about. The matter of divorce is so personal that it seems to be nobody else's business to make judgments…except the two people who made the decision to get married in the first place!

Divorce presents an ugly picture…so we'll consider some of the bad stuff first…and then some of the good results! If marriage is the union of people who really like each other better than anyone else, why should they be expected to stay together if they no longer have that feeling? The whole marriage act is too personal and great a thing to be engaged in by people who no longer like each other, for reasons usually known only by the two of them…and really by no one else! Think of some of the conditions these unions were entered into… the result of a short acquaintance, or a few minutes of intense passion in the automobile or motel, or the traumatic announcement by one of your children that a grandchild is on the way, or just the plain old marriage but without first getting to know each other as they really are! After decisions made under such doubtful circumstances, the world expects two people to stay together for life by 'working it out' regardless of the unhappy situation! Do we think that two people are smarter in this choice for life category than they are with some of their other decisions in life? How often are people scared to death to divorce for family, financial, social, religious, etc., etc. reasons. It's a matter of starting all over with new family, new friends, new finances… really frightening enough to make one wonder how many people who don't get divorced are held together by just plain fear of the consequences. It's not an easy ordeal…a very miserable experience…and all a result of being married!

Now putting all those bad thoughts about divorce aside for a minute…what good can come from such an apparently awful event? Two people not liking each other can rid themselves of hours, days, weeks, months and many years of a miserable existence that was meant to be a very pleasant experience in the beginning. Both parties can get on with their life as an individual, or find that person whose relationship gives a whole new meaning to what life can really be like. People shouldn't have to spend a lifetime adjusting to a constant atmosphere of dislike and distrust of a partner. All of us should be an individual on our own terms…and then if we're lucky, maybe find that certain person who lets us be an individual first…and then just enjoy helping each other be that person. No matter what the pain and cost of divorce may be, the resulting benefits can bring one to a realization, maybe for the first time in life, of what true happiness is all about! Think about it!

Sex and Sexuality

I've read a lot, listened a lot, wondered a lot, passed a lot of exams, and supposedly knew enough of what I was supposed to know. I guess I always believed that I really didn't know what I was talking about… especially enough to be a teacher, counselor, pastor, and whatever else I was called upon to be! Now with all this accumulated education and experience of seventy-five years, I still don't feel any more of an expert…but I sure have a lot of thoughts since I feel free to think about it. I'm going to try not to give this subject any more attention than it deserves…maybe the world has already given it too much attention!

I don't know enough about how sex is thought of in other countries, but in America and our upbringing, I can't help but believe that sex is much too exaggerated. Maybe it gets much too much attention because of the manner in which we shy away from treating it as a normal part of our being. As we're growing up, we learn and speak so plainly about eyes that see, ears that hear, a nose that smells, skin that feels, hands and feet that move, nails, hair, brains, bones, etc., etc., etc. But when it comes to such parts as penis, vagina, breasts, rectums, etc., we seem to have been taught and come up with hundreds of different words to strangely describe them and their functions! Do any of us believe that these are really 'bad things' when we stop to consider their function in our life? We even extend our funny kind of speech to acts of elimination of bodily wastes, apparently because they are so closely positioned and related to 'sex' parts. Where did all this stuff start?…and for what reason?

The legendary 'Adam and Eve' seem to get blamed for most of our attitude towards sex…supposedly covering themselves out of a sense of shame…perhaps believing all those parts 'dirty' thereafter. All kinds of serious temptations to 'sin' result, supposedly, from some act of disobedience. This appears to be the teaching of the Bible and the church, and since I have trouble attaching much belief to either source, I need to find some other reason. How about since some parts of the body aren't all that desirable to look at, man and woman just began to cover those parts? I really believe we do each other a favor by covering ourselves, especially after having been in the nursing home business so long? Just try to imagine walking down the street, conducting business without covering our bodies. This makes clothes a kind of practical matter instead of hiding 'tempting and sinful' parts. The language we use only serves to create a serious attitude of curiosity for children, who then carry such ideas into adulthood. Because of this wrong notion of sex and 'over-curious' emphasis, we see a lot of sex abuse and undue concern about a part of our life that ought to be just as natural to us as seeing, hearing, breathing, etc., etc. That's what I've been thinking for a long time!

And now how about all the different forms that sex takes on in our world today? How about the so-called 'problems' of birth control, homosexuality, masturbation, unmarried couples, etc., about these matters, when our judgment might tell us to use these sexual parts with the same good sense that we use all the other parts of our body. Why shouldn't that work? When I think of the sexual problems I've experienced in my own life, and then add all the sexual problems of other people that I've dealt with through the years, it really makes me kind of sick.

Maybe that's enough about this subject! I believe we need to convince ourselves that sex is good, to be used certainly for more than just bringing children into this world. We don't need to judge those who enjoy sex with themselves, or with others of the same sex, or in an unmarried situation. Maybe it's time to question who the real authority on this subject is! It certainly has caused big problems in the world today, and maybe we ought to do some changing in our thinking and teaching. Think about it!

Gift-Giving, Presence, Presents

Think about it! The number of hours and days and weeks that are spent in the process of deciding what kind of gift to get for some next occasion would add up to an amazing total. It may not seem like much of a topic to write about, but maybe after you finish reading whatever I have been thinking about this matter, you just might wonder, too!

I believe that too much human activity is aimed at one major goal…the attainment of as much money as can possibly be accumulated in one's total worth! If that is the case, then commercial advertising is perhaps one of the best ways to help achieve such a goal…and in what other field of endeavor is the art of advertising more active than in the whole matter of gift-giving?

Newspapers, television, radio and billboards become a constant reminder to us of our next 'obligation' not to forget the next occasion at hand. The business world seems to thrive on inventing more of these occasions as time passes by…and just to name a few…Christmas, birthdays, anniversaries, valentine's day, mother-father-grandparent days, easter, thanksgiving, graduations, weddings, going-away, housewarmings, get well, etc., etc., etc. Because of this constant bombardment by the advertising media, a great amount of stress is added to our lives. A sense of guilt is developed and in some cases a strain on the financial budget that leaves people in miserable debt…such as the after-Christmas blues that takes the minimum wage earner much too long to recover from! These thoughts are mine from experience, both in my own personal bank account and the bank accounts of employees over a period of forty years.

What does this all mean in our life? Well, again I just can't hardly get these words typed fast enough to tell you what I think! I believe so much of this is tied to a mistaken notion of what happiness is all about…and what 'doing for and giving to' others should mean in our lives. I've been thinking for years that people who are grateful for 'what they have' and don't worry so much about 'what they don't have' are the happiest. Whenever we're thinking about the 'good' things, we need to be grateful for what we 'have', and not worry so much about all we 'don't have'. Whenever we're thinking about the 'bad' things, we need to be grateful for the bad things we don't have…we shouldn't have any trouble thinking about all the people who are much worse off than we think we are!

Are you agreeing or disagreeing yet? So what does this all have to do with presents? I really believe good acts and gift-giving are best done anytime we have the urge to do so, not when somebody else tells us to do so. Look at the results in our closets, drawers, basements, attics and garages, that are full of so much unused stuff that needs to be moved around or put on garage sales, because we really have no use for so much. Who hasn't witnessed the disappointment of someone who received too little, or not the right thing, or the child who opened his Christmas present, threw the contents aside and played with the box instead? All of this seems to be so much the result of tradition…and advertising, especially the kind of advertising that appears so many months in advance of the occasion!

So what's the solution? Well, maybe we just ought to start being more grateful for each other's presence… and just let that be our source of joy. Most of us have more than we 'need' already…and what gift is really good enough for the one person who means more to you than anyone or anything in the world? Most of us do about all we can manage for our children already. So my conclusion is…isn't our 'presence' really the important thing for happiness?…and not our 'presents'? If somebody doesn't really enjoy our 'presence', why do we stay around? Why not just stay away and leave them alone? That applies to family, relatives, friends… there's a whole bunch of nice people out there in the big world, who are ready to accept us 'just the way we are', who really enjoy our 'presence' and don't require the 'presents' in order to be happy with us around!

We have so much to be grateful for! Isn't it a shame to let the business world hoodwink us into believing that we can't live without so many things?…besides putting the guilt trip and stress on us throughout the year? If we want to be free human beings, why do we let others control us like this? Think about it!

Timely Preparations

Think about it! I believe someone once said that he was not afraid of death…it's the dying that scared him! We may not be sure of many things in life, but we can all pretty much agree that all of us are destined to die sometime. And none of us knows much about when that sometime will be, unless we are the cause of our own death. With that in mind, it would probably be a bit wise on our part to give some thought and attention to what is going to happen to us and our stuff and the ones we leave behind. These are kind of somber thoughts, but since we are almost positive our time is coming, no matter what age we are at present, getting ready for the event seems like a rather smart thing to do!

Here are some ideas about final wishes, organ donation, cremation, funerals, suicide and cemeteries that you might like to agree or disagree with…one can't help but give a little consideration to these subjects if you think about the matter of dying. Procrastination is very easy to indulge in with these matters on tap…but once the task is completed, one can breathe one of those big sighs of relief that you've accomplished something very worthwhile. It can mean a lot more to your spouse, family, relatives and friends at the all important later date! Having been in the priesthood for several years and in the nursing home business for several more years, you can imagine a considerable amount of experience with death.

Final wishes are a very handy matter to have expressed on paper…when we come to a time of 'losing control' of our own life, someone needs to step in and take over. Maybe you've had that unpleasant task with someone in your own life…and what a relief it is when foresight was actually put onto paper. This is perhaps one of the greatest favors we can do for those whom we trust will follow through with whatever is necessary. Probably one of the scariest things about all of this is making it too formal a process, so we keep putting it off instead of just getting on with it. The most important thing seems to be to do it, not the exactness and formality. The people we entrust ourselves to just need to be informed of our thoughts, and a secure place for our final wishes on paper, such as a security box at the bank.

How about organ donation? If our bodies can be of some use to the living, doesn't it make sense to give a good organ to someone who is waiting for such a donor? As for the rest of our body, research hospitals are able to use our remains for the good of humanity. It seems we could accomplish one more good for humanity, rather than bury our body for no purpose.

Cremation is a natural follow-up to the donation of our body. Some people don't like the idea of cremation, but there are some considerations that make the process thoughtworthy. Some parts of the world make it necessary where burial in the ground is not possible. Another supporting factor is that burning is considered one of the most respectful ways of disposing of sacred, revered or blessed objects…and doesn't the body fit into that category?

Cemeteries don't appeal too much to me…if you've ever had the job of cleaning one, you get very well acquainted! Placing the deceased body of a loved one six feet under the ground forever is a rather dreadful thought. Some people think it's a necessary procedure… burials at sea, earthquakes, fires, plane crashes, wars… all take away the possibility of 'visiting' the deceased after death. Maybe cemeteries are somewhat a waste of space!

Suicides have a general tendency to be frowned upon, but maybe there is room for thought. I believe that some people in nursing homes literally starve themselves to death…and maybe that's not all that bad, if bad at all. The last days of many people are spent in terrible condition…either mentally or physically. Does it seem humane to allow our family members to lie and suffer for so long…when if one of our pets were in such a condition, we would quickly put them out of their suffering? Maybe everyone needs a nursing home experience to be convinced. It's easy to forbid mercy-killing if one has never been involved with a personal experience. Finally we have to come face-to-face with the ultimate question of who says it's wrong to take one's life…who really knows?

And now the subject of funerals! With all due respect for funeral directors, past and present, I think of funerals, with all their trimmings, as a business that has expanded far beyond the good that may have once been present. I believe we might be better off with eliminating the whole period of wakes, memorial services, burials, and whatever else strings out the tough days of grieving endured by the family of the deceased. The expenses alone connected with such occasions are enough to stress some families. The whole scene can be replaced with a decision to donate the organs and body, cremation and no service.

Maybe families who have been through both types of experience at funeral time would be the best to contact to help in the making of your important final days decisions. Think about it!

Conclusion

Some of you might be wondering what I'm thinking now about life, etc. I believe Henry David Thoreau wrote that theology is really natural philosophy…I agree! I believe Thomas Paine wrote that the word of God is creation…not anything written or oral…I agree!

I believe there must have been a first cause or creator or god or power or force that brought about this wonderful world…I'm still having trouble figuring out the "no beginning part" and "why we don't know for sure" about such an important matter! Just have to keep thinking!!

Printed in the United States
69367LVS00001B